Original title:
Laughs Among the Leaves

Copyright © 2025 Creative Arts Management OÜ
All rights reserved.

Author: Colin Leclair
ISBN HARDBACK: 978-1-80567-203-6
ISBN PAPERBACK: 978-1-80567-502-0

Frolicsome Froths of the Foliage

In the woods, a dance unfolds,
Tickling branches, secrets told.
Squirrels chase with comical glee,
A wobbly fox, quite a sight to see.

When rain drops play a joyful tune,
Puddles mirror a cheeky moon.
The rustling grass begins to sway,
Nature's laughter brightens the day.

Happy Reflections in the Rustic Realm.

Sunlit meadows, nature's stage,
Critters troupe, out of their cage.
Bunnies hop in a silly race,
While deer prance with a lively grace.

Crickets chirp in offbeat rhyme,
Field mice dance, forget the time.
Each rustle holds a jolly jest,
In this realm, we find our best.

Whispers in the Wind

The breeze carries a playful tease,
Through tangled branches, it weaves with ease.
Leaves spin like dancers in delight,
As shadows jiggle in fading light.

Owl's hoot bursts like laughter clear,
While chipmunks plot with nibbles near.
A ticklish touch sweeps through the air,
Joyfully echoing everywhere.

Giggles Beneath the Canopy

Underneath the leafy dome,
Whimsical critters make their home.
A raccoon with a mask and flair,
Pulls off pranks with a cheeky stare.

Sunbeams peek through, rays of gold,
Every ripple, a story told.
Nature chuckles, a vibrant sound,
In this world, pure joy is found.

Fun Beneath the Pine

Beneath the pine, a squirrel prances,
Chasing shadows, taking chances.
Leaves are rustling with delight,
As he tumbles and takes flight.

A group of birds joins in the game,
Singing tunes, with no one to blame.
They squawk and hop, what a parade,
Nature's antics never fade.

Cheery Notes in the Understory

A raccoon dips into a snack,
Chips on his paws, no sign of lack.
He winks and giggles with a grin,
As if joy is just a whim.

Nearby, a rabbit does a jig,
Twisting and turning, oh so big!
With every hop, the laughter spreads,
Among the greens, where joy treads.

Giddy Moments in the Canopy

The branches sway, a playful tease,
Monkeys swing with such great ease.
Their chatter echoes, far and wide,
In this playground, they take pride.

A hippo slips on muddy ground,
With a splash, he spins around.
The trees all chuckle, leaves unfurl,
As the joyous chaos starts to whirl.

Jovial Journeys Through the Brush

Through thickets dense and foliage bright,
A hedgehog rolls, a funny sight.
He bumps and tumbles, finds his way,
In this wild dance, he wants to play.

As crickets chirp their silly tunes,
The stars peek out and wink at moons.
What fun it is, this lively spree,
In nature's heart, where we're all free.

Chuckles among the Branches

Up in the trees, a squirrel prances,
Tickling the air with clever glances.
A parrot squawks a cheeky tune,
While dancing shadows swing and swoon.

Rustling leaves, a giggle flows,
As playful winds tease pets and toes.
The branches sway, they twist and twirl,
Nature's jesters in a whirl.

A raccoon peeks with mischief bright,
Stealing snacks under the moonlight.
The branches shake with fits of glee,
In this woodland comedy.

With every rustle, a secret shared,
Laughter blooms, the world's unprepared.
From twig to trunk, a joke unspools,
Nature's stage, where wonder rules.

Playful Breezes

Whispers ride the playful air,
Winds blow softly with flair.
Dandelion seeds float near,
Each drift a tickle, fun and cheer.

A butterfly flutters, light and spry,
It winks at daisies, oh, my, oh my!
Gentle breezes giggle low,
As petals dance, putting on a show.

Tree limbs sway, a wobbly jig,
A sprinkle of joy, a hint of big.
A breeze can tease, it swirls and sways,
Tickling the grass on sunny days.

Listen close, the world's in jest,
Nature's humor, at its best.
In every sigh, a chuckle hides,
For those who wander with open eyes.

Serenade of Sunlit Smiles

Beneath bright skies, the flowers beam,
As sunlight weaves a happy dream.
Petals flutter, laughter swirls,
In this garden, joy unfurls.

A bumblebee, with wobbly flight,
Sips sweet nectar, what a sight!
It hums a tune, a merry game,
Tagging blooms, all the same.

With every sunbeam, chuckles rise,
A symphony beneath the skies.
As nature's choir sings on high,
Smiles spread wide, like wings to fly.

The breeze carries whispers bright,
Of jokes exchanged in pure delight.
In this glade, where sunlight glows,
Happiness seeds, and friendship grows.

Jests in the Garden

Among the rows, a gnome grins wide,
Watching flowers with silly pride.
A hedgehog sings a tuneful tale,
While daisies nod and tiny snails.

The garden gate creaks in mirth,
Welcoming all to joyful earth.
With petals bright and colors bold,
A world of humor, pure and gold.

Ladybugs dance, a polka parade,
While shadows play in sunlit glade.
Each little critter brings a cheer,
In this landscape, laughter's near.

So join the fun, don't hold back,
In this paradise, find your knack.
Nature's jesters all around,
Amusements bloom from ground to ground.

Snug Delights in the Underbrush

In the shade where shadows play,
Squirrels dance in a clumsy way.
A rabbit trips over a patch,
Bouncing back with a funny scratch.

Beneath the ferns, a secret slip,
A hedgehog gives the best of quips.
Mice giggle in their little spree,
Napping under the oaktree.

Hilarity on the Hillside

Up the slope, the breeze does tease,
Rolling hats off heads with ease.
A goat that's stuck in a rickety heap,
Sings a tune that makes us weep.

The flowers sway and dance so bold,
Tickling noses, stories told.
Butterflies join in the fun,
Chasing shadows 'til the day is done.

Whimsy Among the Woods

In a nook where whispers cheer,
A bear tries to juggle, oh dear!
With paws so big and nose so round,
The laughter here is quite profound.

Owl delivers jokes on high,
Causing little birds to cry.
Mushrooms giggle, sprightly and bright,
In this wild and joyous light.

Elation in the Evergreen

Under pines so tall and grand,
A raccoon leads a merry band.
They frolic, tumble, and fall with glee,
Making mischief beside the tree.

A fox with flair, wearing toes like shoes,
Steals the spotlight, spreads the good news.
Laughter echoes with every cheer,
In this green dream, we hold so dear.

Laughter's Melody in the Grove

In a grove where giggles thrive,
Squirrels dance, keeping vibes alive.
Bushes rustle, secrets share,
Echoes of jest float in the air.

Chirping birds join in the fun,
Mocking each other, one by one.
Leaves quiver with every jest,
Nature's joke—a perfect quest.

Breezes tickle the flowers bright,
As shadows move in delight.
Even the brook has a chuckle,
With ripples that make hearts snuggle.

Under the sun, the world seems gay,
Where joy finds a place to play.
In every crack and rustle clear,
Laughter lingers throughout the year.

Mirthful Moments on the Trail

Stumbling footsteps, a playful chase,
Each twig snapped brings a smiling face.
Laughter echoes through the trees,
Even the ants seem to tease.

A stumble here, a trip there,
Nature's humor fills the air.
Giggling mushrooms sway with grace,
In this woodland, joy has a place.

Blossoms wink beneath the sun,
Each petal whispers, 'Join the fun!'
With laughter's charm they softly sway,
Turning each moment into play.

Tracks of laughter leave a trail,
Where webs of jest never fail.
In this space, bright hues abound,
Mirthful moments dance around.

Revels of the Woodlands

In the heart of the woodlands bright,
Creatures gather in merry sight.
Hopping rabbits, a clumsy crew,
Share giggles in a playful brew.

Every branch holds a gleeful tune,
As shadows play beneath the moon.
Frolicsome foxes dart and weave,
While chattering birds up high believe.

The wind carries whispers of glee,
Bringing laughter from tree to tree.
Every leaf becomes a feather,
Shimmering light—a merry tether.

Here, the woods come alive each day,
With nonsense games and light-hearted play.
In the revels where all hearts bound,
Joy paints the forest all around.

Glee upon the Ground

Beneath the sky, where spirits soar,
Tiny feet tap on the forest floor.
A playful breeze, a fluttering sound,
Brings forth the joy that's tightly wound.

Mossy carpets hold giggles still,
As critters scamper, chasing thrills.
Mirthful echoes, soft and light,
Dance like fireflies in the night.

Fungi pop up, like smiles they gleam,
In this world, life is but a dream.
Insects waltz with perfect grace,
Nature's jest, a cheerful embrace.

The laughter spreads, a joyful band,
In every corner, sweet and grand.
With every step, joy seems profound,
Finding glee upon the ground.

Merriment in the Nature's Nook

In a glade where whispers play,
The squirrels dance in bright array,
They twirl and leap with pure delight,
Chasing shadows, taking flight.

A rabbit trips upon a stick,
A gentle thump, the moment's quick,
With twitching ears, it looks around,
And feels the laughter in the ground.

The chirping birds join in the cheer,
With silly songs that all can hear,
They flutter 'round, a joyful sight,
As giggles spread from day to night.

Each breeze that blows brings playful cheer,
The rustling leaves are music clear,
In this nook where smiles partake,
Nature's fun is never fake.

Bursting Joys Along the Path

On winding trails where flowers peek,
The butterflies begin to speak,
With colors bright, they swirl and glide,
A silly painter's joy with pride.

A hedgehog rolls, and tumbles too,
Unruly legs, a comical view,
As snickers rise from bees nearby,
Their buzzing chorus takes to the sky.

Beneath the arching, leafy trees,
The giggles mix with morning breeze,
Each happy footstep brings a grin,
As sunlight plays, inviting in.

With every turn, the laughter grows,
The little stream shares all it knows,
In nature's mirth, we find our way,
Where joy and wonder dance and sway.

Gleeful Murmurs in the Meadow

In a meadow bright with golden rays,
The daisies nod and sway in plays,
A bumblebee performs a jig,
With twinkling eyes, it must be big.

A puppy bounds, so full of glee,
Chasing tails beneath the tree,
Each bound brings chuckles from the crowd,
As they cheer, the smoke turns proud.

The clouds roll by, a fluffy team,
A cheerful race—a sunny dream,
While grasshoppers join in the show,
With jumping starts and leaps to flow.

The sun sets low, the colors blend,
In this laughter, we transcend,
A day well spent with friends around,
In nature's joy, pure bliss is found.

Capering Shadows on the Forest Floor

In the forest where shadows twine,
The ferns wave gently, looking fine,
A wobbly squirrel does a spin,
Its acrobats make laughter win.

Amidst the roots, a creature peers,
With wide, bright eyes and merry cheers,
As rabbits hop, they nudge and groom,
Creating mischief in the gloom.

The owls chuckle on their perch,
As crickets croon, their rhythms search,
Each rustle brings an echo loud,
Of giggles shared, a merry crowd.

When moonlight blankets every nook,
The forest's heart begins to cook,
A joyous ball where antics soar,
In capering shadows, life's never a bore.

Whirling Delights in the Dust

In the sunlit glade, where the breezes play,
Whirls a silly bug, in a clumsy ballet.
The butterflies giggle, twirl in parade,
As the grasshoppers hop, with their grand charade.

Beneath the old oak, where shadows tease,
A squirrel steals snacks, with nimble ease.
He trips on a root, makes a comical sight,
And the woodland erupts in a fit of delight.

The daisies pick up on the growing fun,
Dancing in circles, under the bright sun.
The rustling leaves chime, with whispers so sweet,
As the tiny ants march, and tap tiny feet.

In this joyful corner, where giggles abound,
Each petal and twig shares the mirth all around.
A tapestry woven, with laughter and play,
In the heart of the forest, they celebrate May.

Cackles by the Stream

By the bubbling brook, where the ripples sing,
Frogs in tuxedos leap and spring.
With a plop and a splash, they ponder a dance,
Their croaks turn to cackles, a comical prance.

The fish poke their heads, curious and bold,
While dragonflies flutter, their tales unfold.
A tangle of reeds sways, tickled by cheer,
As the frogs share a joke, it's the best of the year.

The sunbeams cloud over, casting shadows wide,
But the laughter rolls on, like an unstoppable tide.
A raccoon joins in, with his cheeky grin,
As the whole stream erupts in a whirlwind of kin.

So, gather your friends, and come join the fun,
Where the water and laughter gleam under the sun.
In this merry spot, where the humor does gleam,
We'll wade through the chuckles beside the bright stream.

Nature's Jest in the Glen

In the cheerful glen, where the flowers bloom,
A fox trots along, puffed with room.
He slips in the grass, raises quite a stir,
As the daisies chuckle, and the daisies purr.

Up high in the branches, the crows start to squawk,
Making rhymes and riddles, a sarcastic talk.
While the playful breeze sends the leaves in a whirl,
Nature's mischievous grin gives a playful twirl.

Beneath the blue sky, where silliness reigns,
The butterflies flirt, engaging in strains.
Tickling the blossoms, they whirl in delight,
Oh, the giggles of nature, pure joy in sight!

In the heart of the glen, such laughter can't cease,
A festivity born from this devil-may-care peace.
Come lend your own chuckle, join in the jest,
For where joy and mischief meet, we're truly blessed.

Tittering Among the Twigs

In the dappled shade, where the branches sway,
Tittering critters come out to play.
Tiny chipmunks with their whiskers so neat,
Launch an acorn, and look at their feet!

The thrush in the thicket whistles a tease,
As a mischievous breeze sends leaves on the breeze.
A squirrel does a somersault, clumsy yet spry,
And the twigs crack a joke which makes the birds cry.

The sunlight filters through, casting dazzling rays,
Each critter giggles, oh! How the fun plays!
A rabbit hops in, with a wink and a hop,
Joining the chorus, they burst out with a bop.

Each moment a treasure, in the soft, leafy nook,
Where giggles and tittering compose nature's book.
So dance through the twigs, let delight be your guide,
In this whimsical world, let the fun be your ride.

Bright Whispers in the Thicket

Beneath the shade where shadows play,
Squirrels dance, making a day.
Rustling leaves, they giggle and tease,
Tiny tales riding every breeze.

A chattering robin swings on a branch,
While bunnies in grass do their own little dance.
The sun peeks in with a twinkle and grin,
Nature's secrets shared, let the fun begin!

Mice spin tales of their daring race,
While deer watch on with a curious face.
Each creature joins in, a whimsical spree,
In this charming wood, laughter flows free.

As twilight falls, the sounds start to fade,
But echoes of joy in the thicket parade.
With every rustle, with every sigh,
Bright whispers linger, as night draws nigh.

Smile Stories Beneath the Skyline

Up high, the clouds all gather round,
Painting laughter in shades profound.
Pigeons coo with a cheeky twirl,
As city life spins in a whirl.

Beneath the towers, the park comes alive,
Children chasing, their spirits dive.
A dog steals lunch; what a silly race,
While humans shake heads at the canine's grace.

Picnics turn wild with ants on parade,
Each crumb a treasure, a small escapade.
Laughter erupts as sandwiches fly,
In this funny world, silliness won't die.

As evening wraps the city in gold,
Stories of smiles in whispers retold.
Beneath the skyline, joy takes its place,
In every moment, find a funny face.

Delighted Drifts of the Meadow

In the meadow where daisies sway,
Bouncing bumbles come out to play.
A butterfly flutters, a mischievous flirt,
While ladybugs giggle under their skirt.

Grasshoppers sing in a silly tune,
Dancing with daisies under the moon.
Wiggly worms share their wiggle and jive,
Creating a rumble, oh so alive!

The wind whispers jokes to the tall, green grass,
As sunbeams tickle every creature that pass.
Poppies nod knowingly, tales to unfold,
In this joyful scene, laughter's pure gold.

As shadows stretch long, the sun bids adieu,
Crickets serenade in a night filled with dew.
Delighted drifts of a meadow's delight,
Carry us gently into the night.

Breezy Banter Under the Stars

Under the blanket of night's embrace,
Whispers of giggles in every place.
Fireflies waltz, lighting the way,
While owls hoot jokes, come join the play.

Stars twinkle like eyes full of cheer,
As raccoons plot mischief and sneer.
A gentle breeze carries chuckles and dreams,
Where every shadow hides playful schemes.

The moon struts proudly, a halo so bright,
Catching foxes laughing, basking in light.
In night's cozy arms, the fun never ends,
Each flickering spark, where laughter transcends.

And when dawn tiptoes, soft and discreet,
The echoes of whimsy, a chorus so sweet.
Beneath the vast sky, our hearts will intertwine,
In breezy banter, where stars brightly shine.

Whispers of Joy in the Canopy

In the shade where shadows play,
Squirrels dance, come join the fray.
A chipmunk sings a silly tune,
As breezes chuckle, afternoon.

The branches shake with giggles light,
While butterflies put on a flight.
A weasel sneaks, then trips and rolls,
A tapestry of nature's souls.

The whispers blend, a playful tease,
As rustling leaves begin to sneeze.
The sunshine winks, and clouds parade,
In this grand circus, joy is made.

So come and frolic, join the jest,
In leafy realms, where hearts can rest.
For every laugh in nature's realm,
Is magic found at joy's own helm.

Giggles in the Greenery

Underneath the boughs so bright,
Bunnies bounce, oh what a sight!
A leaf spins down, a wiggly dance,
It trips a fox—a funny chance.

The flowers sway with giggly grace,
As frogs leap high, a silly race.
Ants march on with tiny pride,
While wind whispers secrets wide.

Little critters find their cheer,
With every rustle, joy draws near.
A hedgehog giggles at his spines,
While dancing vines do funny lines.

So chase the sun through gentle trees,
And catch the humor on the breeze.
Let nature's chorus steal your sighs,
In vibrant green, the laughter flies.

Frolics Under the Foliage

In a grove where shadows tease,
Critters play with utmost ease.
A rabbit hops on soft, green grass,
As time zips by and moments pass.

The daisies nod, a joyful crowd,
As chirping birds sing loud and proud.
A little mouse looks up and squeaks,
Joined by laughter that nature leaks.

The squirrels play their acorn game,
While others catch the wild rain fame.
A sleepy bear rolls down the hill,
His snoring echoes, bringing thrills.

So gather 'round this verdant spree,
Where mischief lurks in every tree.
The world spins round in pure delight,
Beneath the leaves, in day or night.

Mirth in the Meadow

In a meadow where flowers bloom,
A curious goat discovers the room.
She prances round, then takes a leap,
A tumble happens—giggles sweep!

The sun shines down, a playful glance,
While bees around the blossoms dance.
A butterfly flutters with a whirl,
As young ones laugh, and twirls unfurl.

There's magic here in every breeze,
As daisies nod with joyful ease.
A playful breeze gives laughter wings,
And each small creature softly sings.

So find your joy in fields so wide,
With grassy patches, come and glide.
In every step, let giggles rise,
In meadows free, where laughter lies.

The Nature of Joy in Sundrenched Spaces

Sunlight dances on the ground,
Bouncing beams all around.
Tiny giggles fill the air,
Nature's joy is everywhere.

Squirrels chase with rambunctious glee,
Whiskers twitching, wild and free.
A flutter here, a rustle there,
Every shadow hides a dare.

Wobbling worms on their muddy path,
Full of secrets and a laugh.
Flowers chuckle, petals sway,
In this lively, sunny play.

Breezy whispers, playful sights,
Puppy paws taking flight.
In this world where joy abounds,
Happiness in each sound.

The Happy Patter of Leaves

Pitter-patter, leaves do fall,
Rustling softly, nature's call.
Dancing down, a swaying cheer,
Whispering secrets, drawing near.

Little critters scurry fast,
Chasing shadows, racing past.
Joyful scribbles in the dirt,
Each adventure, each new flirt.

Sunbeams tickle branches high,
As fluffy clouds drift by.
The world is painted with delight,
Spreading giggles, pure and bright.

Each crunchy step, a playful tease,
A symphony of rustling leaves.
Nature's laughter fills the place,
In every turn, a smiling face.

Wondrous Whirls of Playful Spirits

In the glade, the spirits whirl,
Darting here, a dizzy swirl.
Chasing sunbeams, weaving dreams,
Their laughter flows in joyful streams.

Fluffy clouds play hide and seek,
Gentle breezes tease and squeak.
A leaf spins down, a cheerful flight,
Inviting all to share delight.

Branches sway in friendly fun,
Celebrating the warming sun.
Round and round, they sway and sway,
Time to join this frolic play.

Joyful critters, skits and glares,
Sharing stories, laughter flairs.
In nature's arms, they twirl and prance,
Inviting every heart to dance.

Mirth Among the Branches

Squirrels dance in their finest attire,
Chasing each other, never to tire.
A bird with a whistle, sings off-key,
Making all the critters giggle with glee.

Leaves rustle softly, a ticklish breeze,
Who knew nature had such wild expertise?
The branches sway, a comical sight,
As shadows play hide and seek in the light.

A chipmunk trips over a twig in a dash,
Tumbles and rolls, oh, what a splash!
The laughter of nature, loud and bright,
Echoing through the forest with pure delight.

Flowers sway gently, colored in cheer,
They seem to join in, as if to say, "Here!"
With every soft flutter, and whispering sound,
Mirth fills the air; joy abounds all around.

Frolics in the Flora

Bunnies hop high on green velvet grass,
Skip to the tune that the breezes amass.
Petals spin slowly, a whimsical dance,
Nature's grand party—a frolicsome chance!

A butterfly pirouettes, full of grace,
Chasing the sunlight, a thrilling embrace.
The daisies chuckle, with petals a-twirl,
As ants march straight, in a jolly swirl.

Tall stems bend low, as if to conspire,
With mischief hidden in their leafy attire.
The wind tells a joke, and the flowers all nod,
In this merry wonderland, life is quite broad.

Sun shines down while the world twirls around,
Creating a symphony that's joyously found.
In every green corner, where chuckles abide,
Frolics in flora bring grins far and wide.

Jovial Breezes Through the Trees

In the crisp air, a giggle takes flight,
As branches bend low in sheer delight.
The whispers of leaves, in humorous tune,
Sing tales of merriment, morning to noon.

Two owls perch, with mischievous grins,
Swapping wisecracks as the fun begins.
Their wide eyes twinkle, with secrets to share,
Creating a buzz in the woodland air.

A squirrel with acorns, a jester so sly,
Dropping them gently onto passersby.
Each thud brings a chuckle, a ripple of cheer,
As woodland folk gather, as friends drawn near.

Breezes tumble along, spreading laughter so sweet,
With every soft gust, the fun is complete.
Through trees they frolic, like kids at play,
In this whimsical world, joy rules the day.

Snickers in the Sunlight

Sunlight dapples, a playful embrace,
Bringing out smiles on every bright face.
A ladybug skitters, upside-down dance,
While flowers joke, in a floral romance.

A merry old tree with a gnarled-face grin,
Whispers to flowers, "Oh, let's begin!"
The echoes of chuckles bounce off the ground,
As sunshine tickles all, round and round.

Grasshoppers leap, in a grand fit of sass,
Turning the meadow into a class.
Nature's comedians, wild and free,
Make the sunlight sparkle with pure glee.

With shadows that giggle, and breezes that tease,
Every moment is filled with cheer and ease.
In this sunny arena where joy takes flight,
Happiness snickers, shining so bright.

The Carefree Chorus of Nature's Song

In the sunlight, shadows dance,
A rabbit in a comical prance.
Squirrels chatter, secrets they share,
Tickling breezes tug at your hair.

The brook giggles as it flows,
Whispers of mischief, who knows?
Frogs leap high, with grace so absurd,
Each splash echoes the laughter heard.

Sunflowers sway, with cheeky cheer,
Bowing to butterflies hovering near.
A parade of daisies, wild and spry,
With a wink from the clouds up high.

Nature's stage, a show so free,
Filled with glee and jubilee.
With playful tones, the forest sings,
A chorus of joy that always springs.

Smile-Sprinkled Trails Through the Meadow

On winding paths where daisies peek,
A dandelion whispers, 'Come take a peek!'
The grass tickles toes with giddy delight,
As butterflies flutter, a colorful sight.

Jolly ants march in a tidy row,
Their little dance puts on a show.
A breeze twirls petal, a playful tease,
As birds tell jokes among the trees.

The sun chuckles, warming the day,
While rabbits play hide and seek in the hay.
Every nook filled with cheer and grins,
A hidden world where the fun begins.

Beneath blue skies, the joy extends,
With nature's laughter that never ends.
In meadows bright, let spirits soar,
For every trail is a giggle galore.

The Grinning Grove's Anecdotes

Among the trees, where shadows collide,
A squirrel shares stories, with eyes open wide.
Chirping birds crack up in the song,
In this grinning grove, you can't go wrong.

The wind howls a joke, a gentle tease,
As branches sway with amusing ease.
Owls wink knowingly, in the twilight's gleam,
Chasing the moon in a joyful dream.

Every leaf holds a funny tale,
Of bumbles and tumbles on nature's trail.
The laughter rings, a symphony bright,
In the cozy embrace of soft twilight.

With giggles each time the critters unite,
In the grinning grove, life feels just right.
A tapestry woven with joy and jest,
Where tales bring a chuckle, and hearts feel blessed.

Sweet Mischief in the Forest's Heart

Beneath thick boughs, a ruckus brews,
Where playful shadows tease and amuse.
A raccoon sneaks off with a picnic treat,
While the trees giggle at the sneaky feat.

Frogs make faces by the shimmering pond,
Croaking a tune like a cheeky bond.
Every rustle and tickle, nature's game,
A chorus of chuckles, none feel the same.

Vines twine around like a playful hug,
As critters share secrets, all snug as a bug.
The forest's heart thrums with mirth and cheer,
In mischief's embrace, there's nothing to fear.

A dance of shadows in the fading light,
Where laughter lingers, pure delight.
In this haven where joy takes flight,
Sweet mischief lives in the calm of the night.

Joyful Ribbon of the Wind

The breezy whispers tickle the grass,
As playful squirrels dash and pass.
A dance of shadows, twirling round,
In nature's jest, pure joy is found.

Bright blossoms giggle, colors gleam,
Chasing clouds in a sunlit dream.
Butterflies flutter in silly plays,
Painting smiles on a lucky day.

The branches sway with laughter's song,
While tiny critters join along.
A cheerful rustle fills the air,
As springtime winks without a care.

With every breeze, the world ignites,
In merry hues and playful sights.
Nature's jesters, a joyous crew,
In ribboned winds, our laughter grew.

Gleaming Delight Among the Wildflowers

In fields where wildflowers stretch and sway,
The bumblebees buzz in their vibrant play.
Petals nod and giggle in the breeze,
Sharing secrets with the buzzing bees.

A sunbeam slides down, chasing a shadow,
Tickling tulips, brightening the meadow.
Each bloom a jokester, bold and free,
Winking at the world, just like me!

Dandelions puff like feathery jesters,
Fluffing up laughs with their silly gestures.
With every gust, their jokes take flight,
Scattering giggles, oh what a sight!

In this garden where joy takes root,
Nature's whimsy is absolute.
Gleaming delight in every hue,
Sprinkling smiles, just for you.

The Sprightly Soiree of the Sunlit Wild

In the golden glow of a sunny day,
The critters gather for a wild ballet.
Frogs leap high, with croaks of glee,
While rabbits dance beneath the tree.

A party of laughter fills the air,
With rustling leaves in a carefree flair.
Ladybugs twirl on a bright green leaf,
Rustling giggles beyond belief.

The sun winks cheekily from above,
While woodland creatures fall in love.
Breezes hum a merry tune,
As nature's jesters, they'll dance till noon.

A day of joy, a vibrant spree,
In this wild soiree, come dance with me!
In every step, laughter unfolds,
As stories of happiness are joyfully told.

Echoes of Joy in the Wilderness

Amidst the trees where wild things shout,
Echoes of joy twist in and out.
Squirrels chatter, stirring the leaves,
Spreading tales of playful thieves.

A brook giggles as it flows along,
Telling secrets in a bubbly song.
Crickets chirp in the evening light,
Join the chorus of pure delight.

Fireflies twinkle like stars on the ground,
In a dance that knows no bound.
Frolicsome shadows leap in the night,
With playful whispers that feel just right.

With every rustle, laughter is heard,
In the symphony of the wild bird.
Echoes of joy resonate and thrive,
In this wondrous place, we feel alive.

Revelry in the Rustling

In the trees the whispers play,
Squirrels chase their tails today.
The branches sway with giggles bright,
A dance of shadows in the light.

A breeze tickles leaves up high,
As birds chirp jokes that fly by.
The acorns roll with childish glee,
In this woodland jubilee.

Nuts drop down with little thuds,
Creating chaos, making buds.
The laughter echoes through the air,
Foliage rustles, none can spare.

Each rustling leaf a silly tune,
Underneath the watchful moon.
Nature's jest in every sway,
Brings a smile to greet the day.

Chuckles in the Emerald Boughs

Branches dip and swirl around,
While critters scuttle on the ground.
In emerald boughs, a secret spree,
A chorus of laughter, wild and free.

The sunbeams dance on painted leaves,
As giggling winds play tricks and tease.
A wandering rabbit hops with zest,
In this funny woodland fest.

Each shadow twirls in playful light,
The trees join in, what a sight!
A jolly breeze, a soft caress,
Nature's joy wears happiness.

With every rustle, stories unfold,
Of laughter shared and moments bold.
As daylight fades, the giggles cling,
In every bough, joy's sweet offering.

Joyful Echoes Under the Foliage

Beneath the canopy, tales arise,
With secret secrets in the skies.
The squirrels prance in jubilant play,
Chasing shadows through the day.

Tiny critters make their rounds,
In glades where giggles know no bounds.
A rustle here, a flutter there,
Every leaf a laugh to share.

The petals tap with gentle grace,
Nature's jest, a smiling face.
Whispers twist through the gentle trees,
While petals dance in a playful breeze.

Under the sun, all hearts align,
As fables weave through boughs divine.
Joyful echoes fill the air,
With each new day, we laugh and share.

Playful Shadows in the Glade

In a glade where shadows tease,
Laughter hops on the playful breeze.
Butterflies flutter with cheeky grace,
Spreading delight in this sunny place.

The tall grass tickles little toes,
As merry echoes dance and pose.
A frolicsome deer peeks through the trees,
Finding comedy in the swaying leaves.

With every step, the earth joins in,
A symphony of joyful din.
Little paws scamper on the run,
Making mischief, all in fun.

Among the blooms, the day's a game,
Whispers of joy, no shame or blame.
In the glade, we find our way,
With playful shadows guiding our play.

Hushed Hilarity Amongst Ivy

In the shadows, giggles creep,
Where ivy whispers secrets deep.
A squirrel trips, lands in a heap,
We chuckle while the forest sleeps.

Beneath the canopy so lush,
Tiny critters form a hush.
A toad in socks begins to rush,
His silly dance makes us blush.

Leaves turn over, share their tales,
Of pranks and tricks in breezy gales.
A worm in glasses, how he fails,
With every twist, each giggle sails.

Frogs wearing crowns croak a tune,
As laughter bounces 'neath the moon.
Planting joy, we sow our boon,
In nature's jesting, we attune.

Ecstatic Breezes of Laughter

A giddy breeze begins to play,
With dandelions, they're on display.
They swirl and twirl in bright array,
As giggles follow close in sway.

Fluffy clouds drift by so fast,
One trips and falls, what a blast!
Raindrops pull pranks, a joyful cast,
Each splash ignites a friendship vast.

The sun peeks out with a sly grin,
As playful shadows dance and spin.
A hedgehog wears a hat, not thin,
In this comedy, we all win.

When laughter echoes through the trees,
From every branch, a joyful tease.
The world is light, a perfect breeze,
In these moments, spirits seize.

Offbeat Rambles in the Thicket

We wander paths where flowers pout,
A butterfly winks, there's no doubt.
With every step, our giggles sprout,
As foxes watch, they'll join the shout.

A hedgehog rigs a tiny game,
Who'll leap the highest? What a fame!
Each set of paws, a new claim to name,
With laughter echoing all the same.

A raccoon dons a donning flair,
Stealing apples from a square.
His antics cause a rippling air,
As giggles weave through sunny glare.

We skip and hop through fern and vine,
Our hearts alight, our souls entwine.
Nature's jesters, oh how we shine,
In thickets where the fun's divine.

Flutters of Joy in the Underbrush

In the underbrush, where secrets roam,
A busy bee builds something dome.
He slips and fumbles, oh what foam!
We stifle laughs, our happy home.

A caterpillar spins a tale,
Of grand adventures, o'er hill and vale.
With every wiggle, he starts to sail,
Through leafy lanes, bright green, not pale.

Birds join in with chirps and cheer,
Their lively songs, oh how they steer!
A thump and a bump makes us all near,
In nature's joke, we leave a tear.

With every flutter, joy expands,
Our giggles mingle, nature stands.
In tangled woods, we make our plans,
To dance and laugh with gentle hands.

Sunny Snickers in the Garden

In the garden bright and bold,
Flowers tell secrets, oh so old.
The bees buzz low, with cheeky grins,
While petals dance and sway, like spins.

The daisies giggle, soft and spry,
Tickling the wind as it passes by.
A ladybug, in polka dot vest,
Makes the proud ant feel like a jest.

Sunbeams peek through, casting rays,
Turning the ordinary into playful days.
Each shadow whispers, sharing a jest,
In this patch of green, we're truly blessed.

So let's howl like crows, sing songs of cheer,
With muddy boots and laughter near.
For in this garden, where giggles sprout,
We find our joy, letting joy shout.

Merry Tinkles in the Thicket

In the thicket where the wild things play,
Squirrels chatter, brightening the day.
A rustling leaf lets out a squeak,
While hedgehogs grin, so cozy and sleek.

The shadows stroll, with tales to spill,
Mice twirl proudly, oh what a thrill!
A twig breaks feigning a grand ballet,
As sunlight glimmers, chasing clouds away.

Frogs in the pond croak tunes of glee,
Jumping up high, oh, come see me!
The thicket hums with frolicsome sound,
Where laughter leaps, forever unbound.

So dance with me, in this woodland spree,
With whimsical creatures, wild and free.
For each step taken, a giggle's no sin,
In the thicket's embrace, let the fun begin!

Grins Adrift in the Oak

Under the grand old oak so wide,
A crew of critters gather, side by side.
The branches sway with a knowing glance,
As nuts tumble down, join in the dance.

A raccoon winks from a cozy nook,
While wise old owl reads from a book.
Each turn of page, a chuckle shared,
In this lively tale, no one's prepared!

The breeze brings whispers, tickles our ears,
As laughter bubbles, chasing our fears.
Squirrels scurry, tripping on tails,
While the oak stands witness to merry tales.

So grab a seat 'neath this leafy dome,
Where each chuckle feels like home.
For deep in the roots where laughter's found,
In the oak's embrace, joy knows no bounds!

Frothy Joys of the Forest

In the forest, laughter lingers near,
Where mushrooms giggle and pine trees cheer.
A brook gurgles jokes, it's quite a sight,
As fireflies twinkle with pure delight.

The fox tells tales with a playful twist,
Snakes slither by, unable to resist.
Every rustle holds a punchline or two,
Sprinkling the air with humor anew.

The sun peeks through, playful and bright,
Painting the day with golden light.
With each step, the forest shares a song,
A symphony where all hearts belong.

So come take a stroll, don't be shy!
Join in the fun, let your spirits fly.
In the frothy joys where nature thrives,
We'll weave together our merry lives!

Whimsy Wrapped in Green

In the trees, the giggles play,
Swaying branches dance away.
Squirrels chatter, hidden tricks,
Nature's jests, a bag of kicks.

Sunbeams twirl, a golden chase,
Tickling flowers with rays of grace.
Dancing shadows on the ground,
In this joy, our hearts are found.

Rustling leaves share stories bright,
Of secret games, a pure delight.
Mushrooms giggle, toadstools grin,
Whispers echo—let the fun begin!

As the breeze steals laughter's song,
Every rustle won't last long.
Yet in this wood, with every tease,
We find our joy among the trees.

The Lighthearted Symphony of the Leaves

Gentle breezes, soft and sweet,
Caterpillars shimmy, life is neat.
Crickets chirp their playful tune,
Underneath the laughing moon.

Leaves flutter, a merry flight,
Whispers of cheer in the fading light.
Branches sway to a joyous beat,
Nature's rhythm as souls meet.

Daisies prance with all their might,
In the sun, a sheer delight.
Buzzing bees with merry hums,
Gather nectar, while laughter strums.

Each rustle, a story shared,
In this realm, all hearts are bared.
Here we dwell, in mirth's embrace,
A lightened spirit, a joyful space.

Cheery Whispers in the Woods

Tiny voices skip and play,
Beneath the trees, they find their way.
A squirrel trips, down he tumbles,
While in the dirt, the laughter fumbles.

The brook giggles, sparkling clear,
Reflecting moments filled with cheer.
Mice in costumes, acting bold,
Every tale a joy to be told.

Frogs with crowns, croaking delight,
As butterflies dance in light.
With every step, the forest sings,
Of silly tricks and playful things.

In the shade, we giggle and gleam,
Caught in nature's playful dream.
Among the leaves, the joy expands,
Cheerful whispers, life's gentle hands.

Celebrating Nature's Hidden Smiles

Underneath a leafy hat,
Lies a world of chat and spat.
Beetles march in funny lines,
Spotting ants and their designed signs.

The sun peeks through with cheeky glee,
Winking at the bouncy bee.
Flowers nod in capricious jest,
In this space, we find our rest.

Windy secrets swirl around,
Tickling grasses, laughter found.
Falling twigs and giggles sprout,
Nature's whims, they dance about.

Every moment, a mirthful gift,
Hearts light up, minds start to lift.
Among the blooms, we play and roam,
In this garden, we find our home.

Youthful Exuberance Beneath the Elms

Beneath the elms we jump and sway,
With giggles dancing, come what may.
Climbing high, we touch the sky,
In whispers soft, the breezes sigh.

Chasing shadows, we spin around,
While sunlight glimmers on the ground.
The world as silly as can be,
In our own realm, so wild and free.

Tickling branches brush our cheeks,
Finding joy in jumbled streaks.
Each squirrel grins, the birds all cheer,
For every moment draws us near.

Laughter bursts like summer rain,
We twirl and dance, forget the pain.
With every step, a new surprise,
Underneath these playful skies.

Sparkle and Giggles in the Garden

In the garden where petals play,
Buds burst out like kids at play.
Daisies dance, and so do we,
As honeybees buzz merrily.

A clumsy gnome trips on his hat,
While chuckling mice wiggle and chat.
The sunbeams glint on dew-kissed grass,
And tickles bloom as moments pass.

We race with butterflies in flight,
Chasing rainbows, oh what a sight!
The ladybugs join in our cheer,
Painting smiles from ear to ear.

With every giggle, flowers bloom,
To wrap us up in joy's sweet room.
A chorus sings from leaf to vine,
As laughter twirls like warming wine.

The Mirthful Murmurs of Nature

Nature hums with giggles light,
From dawn until the fall of night.
Rustling leaves with stories share,
While critters dance without a care.

A frog croaks jokes, a fox will grin,
Squirrels race where all begin.
With silly games from tree to pond,
Is this a dream? We can't respond!

The clouds above, they puff and tease,
In gleeful forms, they tease the breeze.
Each ripple giggles in the stream,
Tickling feet, a joyful dream.

When shadows fall, the fun won't cease,
With laughter echoing like a breeze.
A symphony of nature's song,
In perfect harmony, we belong.

Fanciful Frolics in Flora

In a meadow bright and bold,
Where laughter springs like tales of old.
The blossoms wink, the ferns do chuckle,
In hidden nooks, we gleefully huddle.

A babbling brook lets out a snort,
As rabbits race, in joyful sport.
With every hop and every bound,
The mirthful echoes swirl around.

The towering oaks join in our fun,
Their branches wave like arms undone.
We flip and roll beneath their shade,
In this enchanting game we've made.

With petals tossed like confetti bright,
We dance in circles, hearts alight.
In this wild garden of joy's decree,
Each moment crafted so vividly.

Chortles beneath the Boughs

In the canopy, whispers spread,
Squirrels dance, a bustling thread.
Pinecones roll, what a sight,
Nature chuckles, pure delight.

Crickets chirp with a tune,
Under the watchful, silly moon.
Branches sway, giggles arise,
A tickle from the breeze, oh how it flies!

Rabbits hop, dressed in zest,
Their antics, simply the best.
Gnarled roots twist, secrets they keep,
As shadows waltz, the forest leaps!

Laughter lingers, echoes wide,
In this green world, we abide.
With each rustle, joy ignites,
In leaf-strewn paths, the fun invites.

Joyful Rustle of Nature

A brook babbles, full of cheer,
Where frogs croak songs we long to hear.
Dancing ferns, play hide and seek,
Nature's laughter, bursting unique.

Butterflies flit in playful chase,
Creating smiles on every face.
Hummingbirds dive, a dizzying flight,
As petals twirl in pure delight.

The sunbeams beam, quite absurd,
Painting shadows, laughter stirred.
With every rustle, secrets cheer,
Nature's giggles, so near, so clear!

A twist here, a turn there,
Joyful spirits fill the air.
In every nook, a chuckle's found,
While nature's whispers swirl around.

Raucous Revelry of the Forest

Beneath the boughs, a party bursts,
Woodpeckers tap to nature's firsts.
Chattering chipmunks, oh what a scene,
Life in the woods, lively and keen!

Mushrooms dance in the dappled sun,
Every moment, more mischief begun.
The wind tells tales of echoes gay,
As leaves sway gently, in disarray.

A caterpillar spins a yarn,
While ants march in an army, quite the charm.
The world conspires, in fits of glee,
A raucous fair, just wait and see!

Twilight chuckles, shadows and light,
Critters cavort, it's a marvelous sight.
In this wild revel, hearts find a place,
Where joy is a dance, nature's embrace.

Cheerful Echoes in the Thicket

In thickets dense, the echoes ring,
A chorus of giggles that nature brings.
Bushes rustle, secrets unfold,
As stories of laughter are shared, retold.

A rabbit trips, nose all a-quiver,
In puddles of joy, they leap and shiver.
The breeze can't stop its silly play,
Tickling vines along the way.

A flash of feathers, a swoop so sly,
Birds exchange jokes as they fly high.
Squirrels play chase, through branches they dart,
With each tumble, they steal the heart.

As dusk descends, fun takes its stage,
In nature's book, we turn the page.
Through leafy laughter, our spirits soar,
In echoing woods, forever explore.

Elation in the Understory

Beneath the boughs, a giggle grows,
Squirrels tell jokes, while the wind blows.
With every rustle, a chuckle flies,
As sunlight tickles the leafy ties.

Frogs in capers leap with glee,
Whispering tales of a buzzing bee.
Mushrooms giggle, in fungal fun,
As nature winks, the day's begun.

Petals dance with a teasing glance,
The grasshopper hums to the ants' prance.
Amidst the blooms, a jest unfolds,
Every petal a story told.

So join the cheer, don't hesitate,
In shady nooks where giggles wait.
Underneath the laughter blooms,
A world alive with bright costumes.

Whimsical Winds of Wit

A breeze whispers secrets, soft and slight,
Twisting paths in a playful flight.
The branches sway, in a cheeky jest,
Tickling leaves on a leafy crest.

Birds crack jokes with each little chirp,
As blossoms chuckle, and green roots burp.
The old oak grins, with wisdom untold,
While stories of blossoms continue to unfold.

A dandelion floats, a wish in the air,
Making the fairies giggle and stare.
With every tumble, laughter takes wing,
Nature's own stage with a comical fling.

So let's tire the sun with our mirth,
In the heart of the woods, come dance and frolic.
For in the whispering winds that play,
We find joy in the light of day.

Grins through the Glades

In hidden nooks, where light weaves bright,
Joy leaps forth in the morning light.
A bunny hops with a mischievous twitch,
As butterflies flit, in a colorful hitch.

Through tangled vines, a giggle rings,
The chipmunks chatter, and the laughter clings.
With every rustle, the bushes know,
That nature's jesters put on quite a show.

A beetle winks in a shiny coat,
On lily pads, the ripples float.
While the sun beams down and shadows sway,
The forest rejoices in a playful ballet.

So let's roam the glades, our spirits break free,
In nature's circus, you and me.
With every step, surprise waits near,
Amidst the grins, we find our cheer.

Sprightly Shadows Dancing

In the dappled light, shadows weave,
A sprightly jig, they twist and leave.
Around the roots, they skip and twirl,
As breezes play, and laughter swirls.

Mice hold hands with the drifting leaves,
While in between, a chortle weaves.
The thistles poke with a playful dare,
Inviting all to join this affair.

With every flutter, the humor bounces,
As grasshoppers hop and the sunlight pounces.
Giggling ferns in the warmth of day,
Create a world where joy will stay.

So gather near, let spirits sway,
In nature's arms, where jesters play.
For in the shadows, a dance begins,
In delightful steps, our laughter wins.

Jovial Whispers of the Wild

In the grove where giggles play,
Squirrels dance in bright array,
Branches sway with secrets shared,
Nature's jesters, unprepared.

Beneath the boughs, shadows prance,
Lively leaves begin to dance.
A rustle here, a chuckle there,
Laughter floats upon the air.

Bumbles bees with buzzing cheer,
Tickle twigs, oh, what a year!
Witty winds with tales to tell,
As sunshine seems to cast its spell.

Giggling grass and playful vines,
Whispers ignite with punchy lines.
Nature's canvas, bright and bold,
Where every story weaves pure gold.

Hilarity in the Hedges

Beneath the bramble, whispers bloom,
Frogs engage in jovial zoom.
Every twig in cheeky mood,
Shapes a riddle, light and crude.

Winking flowers, petals wide,
Secret jokes that they confide.
A hedgehog chuckles, snug and round,
Nature's jesters abound, abound!

Rustic roots in playful tease,
Swaying soft in the gentle breeze.
With every turn, a giggle leaps,
As the world around us keeps.

Mischief lurks in every nook,
Caught with wonder, take a look!
Laughter blooms on every branch,
In jest, we're taken in the dance.

Sunny Smirks among the Sycamores

In sunlit glades, the laughter swells,
Among the sycamores, tales it tells.
A breeze that teases, sly and spry,
With winks of light that dart and fly.

Squirrels hide in branches high,
Making faces with a sly sigh.
Every rustle, a playful poke,
Echoing giggles, a joyful joke.

Acorns tumble, rolling free,
Bouncing bright, what glee to see!
Nature's glee in vibrant hues,
With every step, a jest ensues.

Sun-drenched afternoons abound,
Where gentle laughter can be found.
Enchanted moments, spirits lift,
As nature gifts us laughter's gift.

Cheer in the Chiaroscuro

In shades of light and shadows deep,
Whispers of mirth begin to leap.
Dappled spots where giggles glow,
Chasing sunbeams, to and fro.

A playful fox with a knowing grin,
Stirs the air as the fun begins.
Carved in bark, a chuckle stays,
In twilight's embrace, it softly plays.

Jestful breezes in twilight time,
Tickling leaves with a chime and rhyme.
Laughter sprouts from roots of cheer,
In a world where whimsy's near.

Glimmers shine in earthy folds,
Each step a tale, a jest unfolds.
Among the dark, the light shines bright,
We dance through shadows, pure delight.

Mischief in the Maple

A squirrel spins tales from above,
Chasing shadows, dreaming of love.
Branches shake with raucous cheer,
Each ripple whispers, 'Come join here!'

The acorns dance a silly jig,
While owls wink from a cozy twig.
The playful breeze runs wild and free,
As laughter echoes, 'Come play with me!'

Gaiety of the Glades

A rabbit hops with goofy flair,
Ears flopping as he darts through air.
Beneath the boughs, the shadows prance,
Every leaf joins in the dance.

The sunbeams twinkle, casting light,
A game of hide-and-seek in sight.
With every rustle, giggles burst,
Nature's joke, delighting first.

Lightheartedness in the Leafy Labyrinth

A maze of green leads to surprise,
Where whispers tickle, and mischief lies.
Twisting paths that weave and twirl,
Caterpillars pipe up in a swirl.

Each turn reveals a cheerful sight,
Dances of shadows, pure delight.
Even the branches sway and play,
In this leafy world of endless day.

Delight in the Dappled Light

Sunlight dapples through the trees,
Spinning tales on the gentle breeze.
The flowers giggle, petals bright,
Dancing together in pure delight.

A toad hops in a playful game,
Crowned in dew, never feeling shame.
With every twist, a secret shared,
Laughter abounds, no one is spared.

The Secret Joys of the Blades

In the meadow, whispers flow,
Blades of grass in a playful show.
Twisting, turning, wild and free,
They chuckle softly, just for me.

Beneath the sky, a ticklish breeze,
Teasing strands with joyful ease.
Each step brings a giggle anew,
A secret pact, just us two.

As sunbeams twirl in golden glow,
They dance with shadows, fast and slow.
A game they play, a jolly spree,
Oh, what fun in their company!

So join the frolic, sway and sway,
With blades below, it's a perfect day.
Their sunny secrets, pure delight,
In grassy laughter, hearts take flight.

Playful Tricks in the Timber

In the woods, where shadows play,
Trees giggle softly in their sway.
Branches shake with a playful jest,
A trunk hides secrets, never rests.

Squirrels scamper, quick and spry,
Nuts a-flying, oh my, oh my!
Leaves rustle with a teasing tease,
Nature's pranksters, feel the breeze.

A twig snaps loud, the laughter grows,
As sunlight dances, friendship shows.
Among the pines, the fun's alive,
In each embrace, the spirits thrive.

So hear the tales the forest tells,
Of lighthearted pranks, and playful spells.
With every step, let joy cascade,
In the timber's heart, we're unafraid.

Cheerful Rambles Through the Vale

In the vale where daisies twirl,
Joyful breezes lift and swirl.
Butterflies giggle, darting bright,
A cheerful path that feels so right.

With every step, the earth does sing,
Songs of joy and playful spring.
Peeking through flowers, a bunny prance,
In this charm, we take a chance.

The hills echo with happy sounds,
Laughter rolling over mounds.
Each pebble tells a tale of glee,
In this vale, let's roam carefree.

So take my hand, let's run and play,
In the golden light of day.
Here in laughter, let's reside,
Where cheerful moments swell with pride.

The Amusing Dance of Dappled Sun

The dappled sun begins to prance,
With flickering rays in a merry dance.
Warmth spills laughter across the land,
As shadows wiggle, hand in hand.

Beneath the trees, the games ignite,
Sunbeams chase and share delight.
The grass is tickled, the flowers sway,
In this lively, sunlit play.

Every glimmer a giggle pure,
Nature's joy, a sweet allure.
With every twinkle, spirits soar,
In this bright gleam, we'll laugh some more.

So let us twirl in golden glows,
As nature's humor joyfully flows.
In this dance, let hearts unite,
In the amusing warmth of light.

Blissful Banter in the Wilderness

In the forest's gentle embrace,
The squirrels tell jokes at a lively pace.
Rabbits chuckle, rolling in the grass,
As sunlight wiggles, letting joy amass.

A wise old owl hoots puns from high,
While butterflies dance, wings fluttering by.
The brook gurgles tales of silly delight,
As nature's humor takes joyful flight.

Breezes carry whispers, cheeky and bold,
Laughter ripples in stories retold.
Each tree wears a grin, a knowing flair,
In this wild expanse, fun fills the air.

So come share a chuckle, delight in the fun,
Where merry creatures bask in the sun.
In this wilderness, friendship grows steep,
And the laughter of nature is ours to keep.

Smiles in the Shade

Beneath the lush canopy, secrets unwind,
Where shadows of tall trees gift joy undefined.
Jolly grasshoppers leap with delight,
Chirping their songs into the cool night.

A chubby chipmunk, with cheeks stuffed full,
Tells tales of mischief, ridiculous and dull.
The breeze whispers jokes; the leaves seem to quake,
As branches sway gently, a joyous shake.

Every flower giggles, tickled by air,
Petals in motion, a whimsical flair.
Joyful moments in this grove find their way,
As smiles in the shade dance through the day.

Let's lounge in this laughter, under trees so wide,
In this cheerful retreat, let worries subside.
With every soft rustle, a spark ignites,
Playing hide and seek with the day's pure delights.

Jests in the Jumble of Green

In a tangle of emerald vines, out she spills,
A hedgehog with puns and a bag of thrills.
He jabs and he jests, what a sight to behold,
As laughter erupts from the brave and the bold.

The ants form a choir, all lined in a row,
Singing their jingles with a rhythmic flow.
A lizard bright jokes through the dappled sun,
As blossoms giggle, the day's just begun.

A dancing rabbit with a curious spin,
Winks at the crowd with a cheeky grin.
The wind plays along, a merry old tune,
To the rhythm of nature and sweet afternoon.

In this jumbled green, where fun seems to thrive,
Every creature and leaf feels oh so alive.
So join in the jest, let your spirit be free,
In this playground of laughter, just you and me.

Cheerful Whirls among the Blossoms

Dancing petals swirl with a giggle and twirl,
As bees buzz around in a wonderful whirl.
Each flower's a jester, with colors so bright,
They tickle the air, filling hearts with delight.

A chortling brook teases, sparkling and spry,
It whispers sweet stories as it rushes by.
The sun joins the fun, casting playful rays,
While frogs join the chorus in whimsical displays.

Swaying tall grasses sway and conspire,
In the cheerful embrace of warm sunlight's fire.
They join in a jig, every blade in a spree,
Creating a tapestry of joy, wild and free.

Come, frolic in bloom, let your laughter take flight,
In fields of jubilation, from morning till night.
With nature as witness, we dance to the song,
In this blissful gathering, where all of us belong.

Chortles Beneath the Arbor

Squirrels toss their acorns high,
A wiggle here, a tumble shy.
Branches dance with playful glee,
A comedy in every tree.

A robin slips, a branch does sway,
Its feathers puffed, it saves the day.
With each unexpected glide,
Nature and laughter collide.

The breeze runs wild, a ticklish tease,
As leaves perform their jiggly tease.
Whispers of joy in the air,
Every moment, a giggling flair.

Beneath the shade, we pause to share,
A hearty chuckle, a joyous dare.
In every nook, a smile resides,
Where humor in the green abides.

Laughter in the Leafy Embrace

A dandy bug with grand parade,
Struts along the leafy braid.
In shades of green, they twirl and spin,
With every step, a giggle within.

The wind whispers secrets of old,
As blossoms break from their hold.
Petals flutter like silly hats,
Nature's jesters that play with cats.

Bees buzz by with a cheeky grin,
Chasing the blooms to blend within.
They stumble, tumble, down they fall,
A silly dance, a cheerful call.

Underneath the canopy wide,
Humor blossoms, it won't hide.
With every shade, the laughter spreads,
A comedy show among the beds.

Amusement Among the Acorns

A wise old owl begins to hoot,
In mismatched socks and feathered suit.
Then all the critters start to cheer,
As woodland weirdness draws them near.

Chipmunks juggle nuts in sight,
With tiny paws, they hold on tight.
A wobbly show, they flip and fly,
The sun-baked ground, their stage so spry.

Jumping jays in vibrant hues,
Pirouette with silly views.
They chirp a tune, a jolly beat,
As leaves sway low with cheerful feet.

From acorn caps to twinkling eyes,
The laughter swells beneath the skies.
In every nook, the fun persists,
A woodland wonder that can't be missed.

Glee in the Grove

In thickets thick where shadows play,
The blossoms giggle at the day.
A dappled sun begins to wink,
As nature's humor starts to sink.

The rabbits race, a hopping spree,
With floppy ears and giddy glee.
They dash between the roots so grand,
A playful chase across the land.

A chorus of frogs in silly croak,
All join in for the hearty joke.
With each ribbit, another gasp,
How funny life can be with a clasp!

Under the boughs, let laughter steer,
In every leaf, in every cheer.
Nature's stage is set just right,
Where joy and chuckles take their flight.

www.ingramcontent.com/pod-product-compliance
Lightning Source LLC
Chambersburg PA
CBHW072149200426
43209CB00051B/909